Ken Webster
Illustrated by Kris Wuellner

The Tamaroa Village at Grassy Lake

Roxana - South Roxana, Illinois

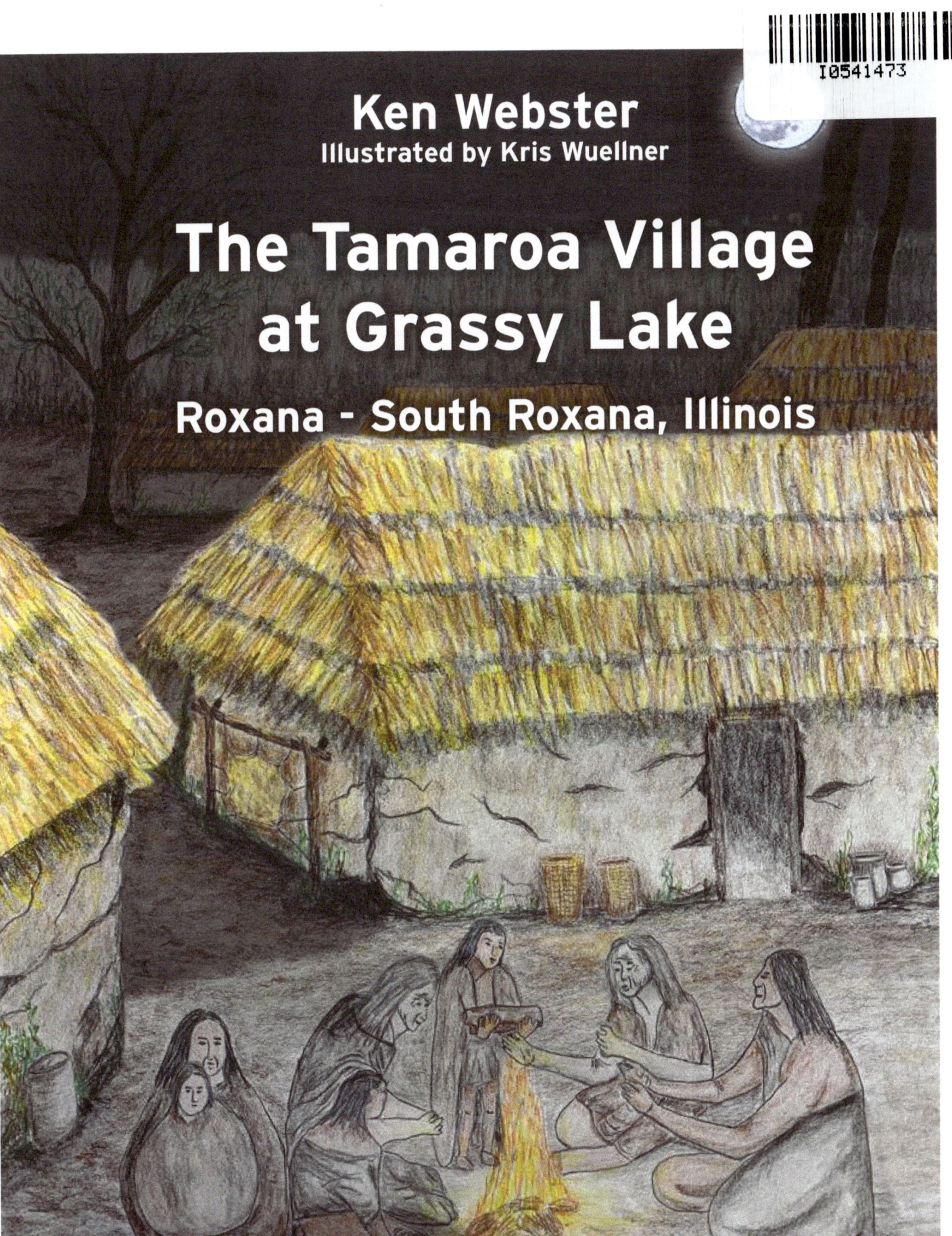

The Tamaroa Village at Grassy Lake
Ken Webster
Russell Four Books

Published by Russell Four Books, St. Louis, MO

Cover and Interior design: Davis Creative Publishing, DavisCreativePublishing.com

Illustrations: Kris Wuellner

Publisher's Cataloging-in-Publication
(Provided by Cassidy Cataloguing Services, Inc.)

Names: Webster, Ken, 1951- author. | Wuellner, Kris, illustrator.

Title: The Tamaroa village at Grassy Lake : Roxana - South Roxana, Illinois / Ken Webster ; illustrated by Kris Wuellner.

Description: St. Louis, MO : Russell Four Books, [2023]

Identifiers: ISBN: 979-8-9894047-0-4 (paperback) | 979-8-9894047-1-1 (hardback)

Subjects: LCSH: Tamaroa Tribe--Illinois--Roxana--History. | Indians of North America--Illinois--American Bottom--History. | BISAC: HISTORY / Indigenous Peoples in the Americas. | HISTORY / North America. | HISTORY / United States / State & Local / Midwest (IA, IL, IN, KS, MI, MN, MO, ND, NE, OH, SD, WI)

Classification: LCC: E99.T18 W43 2023 | DDC: 977.300897--dc23

ATTENTION CORPORATIONS, UNIVERSITIES, COLLEGES AND PROFESSIONAL ORGANIZATIONS: Quantity discounts are available on bulk purchases of this book for educational, gift purposes, or as premiums for increasing magazine subscriptions or renewals. Special books or book excerpts can also be created to fit specific needs. For information, please contact Russell Four Books, kenwebster@yahoo.com.

Table of Contents

Introduction

Imagine that you are driving to Illinois from the Poplar Street Bridge in St. Louis on I-55. You will reach Illinois Highway 111. If you take the exit and go north, you will be heading toward Roxana, Illinois. After the exit onto Rt. 111, look to your right eastward, and you will, no doubt, notice Monk's Mound, the tall central mound from the Mississippian city of Cahokia. If you haven't visited, you should take the time to do so. The Museum Interpretive Center is informative, and the view of other mounds and Wood Henge is magnificent.

Traveling northward for about 10 miles, you will pass Horseshoe Lake State Park, where the Mississippi River changed course. Continuing on, you will pass through Pontoon Beach and finally enter the village of South Roxana. The huge Wood River Oil Refinery will be in view, but also look eastward, toward Daniel Boone Street. A small mound is in view from the highway in the Dad's Club Park, marked with a flag pole and stone War Memorial. This small mound is the single one that remains from Grassy Lake Village, and even it has been eroded over the years. When the refinery was constructed in 1917, all other mounds were removed to prepare for this huge project. Also, take time to notice the small pond to the east and bigger ponds and wetlands to the west. These are remnants of Grassy Lake that curved around where the refinery now stands, preceded by a Mississippian Village of plus or minus 1000 people. The lake was formed when the Mississippi changed course. Passing by the refinery on IL Rt. 111, notice the contour of the land.

The refinery towers and buildings sit higher than the west side of Rt. 111. Although bulldozers have been used to reshape the landscape, there is a natural upward slope, making the refinery site a perfect location for a village for these indigenous people. Grassy Lake, at the base of the village, would have been a source for food and daily needs. In addition, the great Mississippi and Missouri Rivers confluence was not far off to the west, being another natural resource for the needs of the people. Also, there were nearby wooded areas and prairie. The bluff hills in the eastern background are in clear view. The great city to the south, now called Cahokia, would also be near enough to travel for trade. It is no wonder that these early people would have chosen to construct a village at this location.

Mound #10, located at Dad's Park in South Roxana – the only remaining mound from Grassy Lake Village.

2

Who Lived at Grassy Lake Village?

It may be important to point out that no two time lines showing the beginning / ending points of the time periods are exactly the same; however the order and general durations match up. Paleoindians or Paleo-Americans were the first peoples who entered, and subsequently inhabited, the Americas during the final glacial episodes of the late Pleistocene period. Sharpened stone points attached to sticks were used to hunt large ice age animals. They were nomads who did not establish permanent communities.

The period from about 8000 BCE to 1000 BCE is known as Archaic. Early Archaic people continued a nomadic lifestyle, but their stone tools were improved for hunting and gathering. Eventually, people became less nomadic and began to settle into small villages. During this Middle Archaic period, farming methods improved, so they lived as community for at least part of the seasons. By the Late Archaic, approximately 1500 BCE to 500 BCE, people became more skillful for hunting and growing edible native plants, enabling them to develop more specialized methods for community living. Evidence of Archaic people in the Grassy Lake area has been discovered, suggesting the site has been important to indigeous people throughout time.

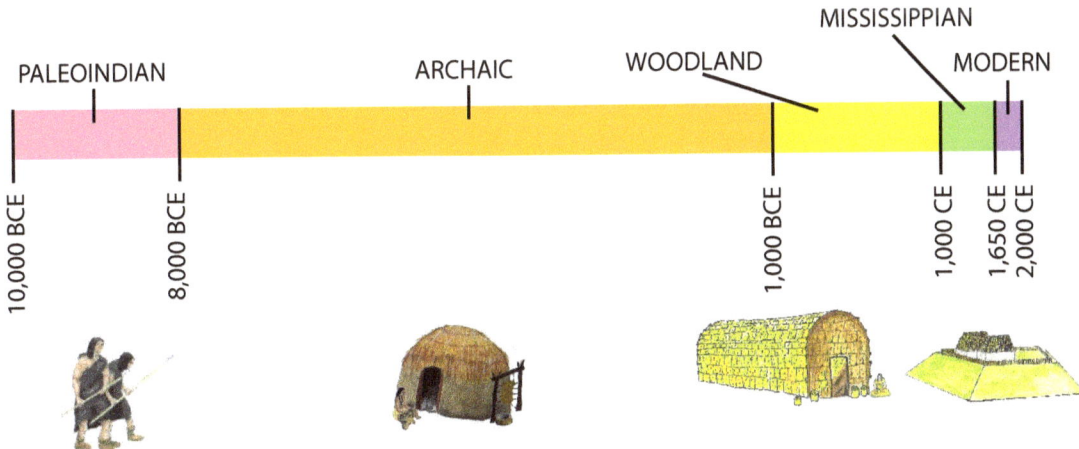

The Woodland period followed, from about 1000 BCE to 1000 CE. As the name suggests, the Eastern Woodland people took their living from the vast forests east of the Mississippi River, and from Canada to the Gulf of Mexico. Deer were important to their way of life, providing food, clothing, and even bone material for simple tools and jewelry. Their villages became more complex than their Archaic ancestors. Since so many trees were around, they learned to make bows and arrows and spears and tools for farming. Bark from trees was used to make bags, dwellings, canoes and baskets. They built framework structures covered with bark, also. Longhouses were so big that several families could live in just one. Other similar structures were used for storage. Village tribes formed larger nations such as the Iroquois, Delaware, Chippewa, Mohegans, and Algonquian. In the south, there were tribes such as Cherokee, Choctaw, Natchez, and Seminole. The Woodland people became good farmers with crops such as corn, squash, and beans. They learned good techniques for fishing and hunting. Furthermore, they became experts on wild plants to use for food, medicine, and basket weaving. They were well established when European settlers began coming to North America.

The Mississippians

Woodland people in the South had begun to build impressive mounds from soil. As time progressed, mound building spread among the culture, especially along the great Mississippi River and its tributaries. By now, methods of farming, hunting, and daily living had become more advanced and villages were established by the Mississippians.

Grassy Lake Village was one of those. Take a look at the map showing the location of the many Mississippian Villages. The information in this book will focus on the one at Grassy Lake, but keep in mind the culture and lifestyle were similar to all Mississippians.

Archeologists categorize Mississippian settlements into 4 tiers: Tier 1 communities were small, without mounds. Tier 2 settlements consisted of several hundred people around a plaza and nearby lake or stream. Tier 3 villages were bigger with populations in thousands with multiple mounds and more complex social structure. A 4th tier would have been very large and a population center for satellite communities – Cahokia. Grassy Lake probably began as a 2nd tier village, approaching a 3rd level one.

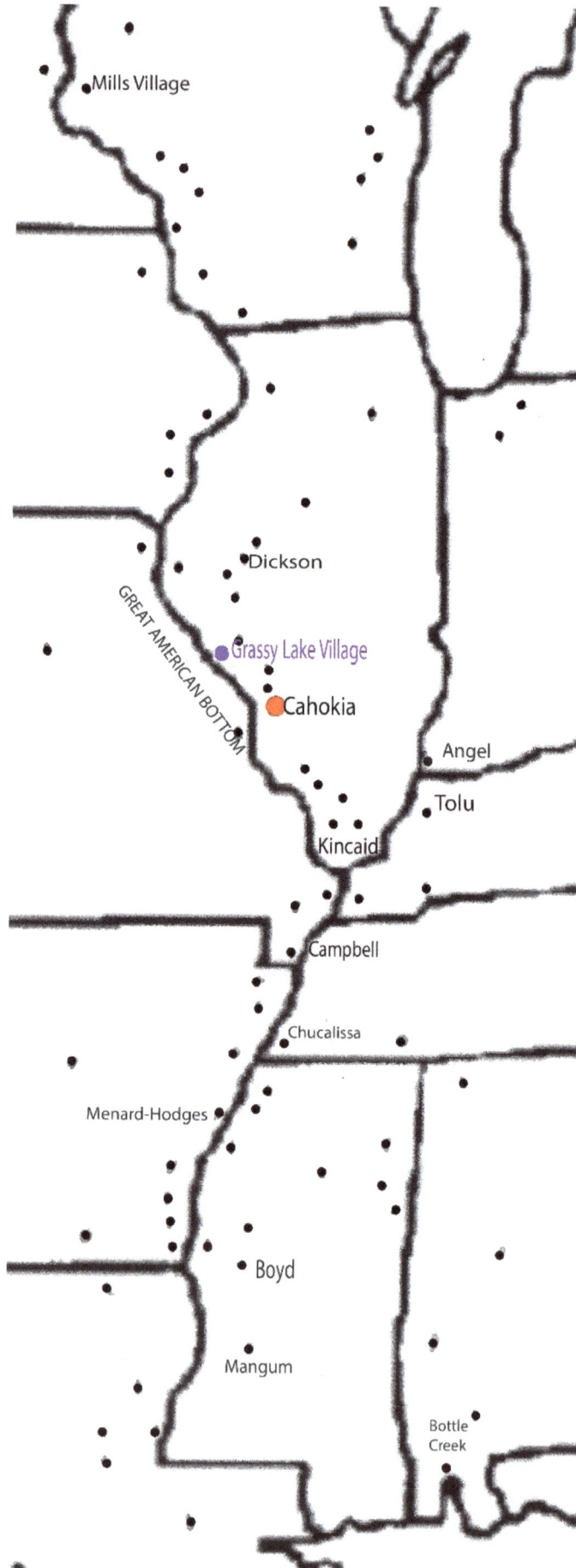

Mississippian People were mound builders. Some of the mounds were built for ceremony, some for burial, some for buildings of important people, and some as boundary markers. Others, known as effigy mounds were even shaped like animals such as birds, reptiles and people. There were no bulldozers, horses, carts with wheels, or trucks. They were constructed by using the tools they had, primarily made of stone, to loosen ground and carry it to the construction site a basket at a time. This was long, hard work, indeed.

*What does BC and AD stand for? And why were they changed to BCE and CE?

Our calendar was based on the birth of Christ; all years before Christ's birth have traditionally been designated B.C. (before Christ) and those after his birth as A.D., an abbreviation for the Latin term "Anno Domini" which means "in the year of the Lord."

Now, scientists and historians have adopted an alternative dating system. They are referring to B.C. as B.C.E. (before the Common Era), and to A.D. as C.E. (Common Era).

The change was made to mask the Christian bias for the dating system, in a bid to accommodate non-Christians and maintain political correctness. Wikipedia

Mounds at Grassy Lake

It is important to note that arbitrarily removing mounds for industrial, business, residential, or agricultural purposes is now illegal at both Federal and State levels. There is respect for the treatment, repatriation, and disposition of Native American human remains, funerary objects, sacred objects and objects of cultural patrimony. There is generally consultation with Native American descendants for advice with such matters.

Since adequate records were not kept, we are uncertain how many mounds existed at Grassy Lake Village; however, there are records and evidence of at least twelve or thirteen. John E. Kelly, Washington University, St. Louis, reports several scenarios based on interviews of local residents, recorded information, including files from the Illinois State Museum. Much of the information in this book comes from Kelly's findings. There is strong evidence that people were active at this site during archaic and Late Woodland / Early Mississippian through time, and most recently, Late Mississippian. The people would have been of the Tamaroa tribe, which were natives who lived near the confluence of the great Missouri and Mississippi Rivers. They were part of the Illinois Confederation, or Illini or Illiniwek, consisting of a dozen or so tribes, all speaking the Algonquian language such as Kaskaskia and Peoria. These Mississippian cultural people rose about 800 CE, but gradually declined and abandoned their villages by around 1350 CE. Also, it is safe to make assumptions about the lifestyle and culture of the Grassy Lake Village based on known lifestyles of similar Mississippian villages. This book focuses on describing the village from a general viewpoint, rather than detailed archaeological studies. However, readers who desire to delve deeper into archaeological studies are encouraged to investigate, especially, reading John E. Kelly's paper included in the book, *Mounds, Modoc, and Mesoamerica – Papers in Honor of Melvin L. Fowler.*

One of the first references to Grassy Lake and the group of mounds was written by William Clark during the time that he and Merriwether Lewis camped near the Illinois side of the confluence of the Mississippi and Missouri Rivers. Along with their crew, they used the fort they had built to camp during the winter months before beginning their famous expedition up the Missouri River to explore the newly acquired Louisiana Purchase. They were at "Camp Dubois" from December 1803 through May 1804. During the time they were there, they scouted the area to learn the land and about any people they encountered. On January 9, 1804, Clark recorded in his journal a description of the mound group east of the camp site.

Although not specifically precise, this journal entry, with grammatical errors and all, gives insight to a possible Mississippian village that preceded European descendant endeavors. There was not much else recorded about the site or mounds during the 1800's, but there were a couple maps drawn of mound locations for the entire region between Cahokia and Alton, known as the American Bottom. Only a couple references to excavations were recorded. On May 11, 1916, The Alton Evening Telegraph, local newspaper, had an article about the site since the oil refinery had begun construction.

Journal Entry made by William Clark on January 9, 1804

"I took Collins and went to the place he found a Hog skinned & hung up, the crows had devoured the meet, Killed Prary fowl and Went across a Prary to a 2nd Bank where I discovered an Indian Fortification, near the Second bank I attempted to cross a Bond of about 400 yds Wide on the Ice & Broke in this fortress is 9 Mounds forming a circle two of them is about 7 foot above the leavel of the plain on the edge of the first bank and 2 M from the Woods & about the Same distance from the main high land, about this I found great quantities of Earthren ware & flints about M. N. is a Grave on an Eminence. I returned before Sun Set."

ALTON EVENING TELEGRAPH

May 11, 1916

A burial place of the original old settlers, antedating the American Indians in Madison County, was today affording interesting study to students of ethnology and archaeology. Workmen excavating on a small hill just inside of the Roxana Oil Refinery at Roxana yesterday unearthed the bones of fifteen skeletons. On previous occasions other skeletons were uncovered in that vicinity and the discovery of the additional skeletons yesterday helps to demonstrate that at some time there must have been many people buried in that neighborhood. Many of the skeletons were found almost whole, in an upright posture in the soil. The skeletons appeared to be both male and female, and of old and young persons. The skulls were well preserved, and the teeth were in good condition. On each of the skulls on the right side there appeared to be a small dent, which might have been made by a savage's war club. The skeletons are not of Indians, for the large jaw bone of the Indian and the large joint bones, which characterize the Indian skeleton are lacking. Ethnologists have frequently declared that at one time a highly developed race lived in America before the Indians, and that they were slain by the Indians.

The finding of the skeletons gives rise to the belief that there must have been a massacre of an entire tribe of highly civilized prehistoric men at that place by the Indians, and that they were all buried together in a heap, which is now the site of the Roxana Oil Refinery [former Shell Oil, now Conoco Phillips, at Hwy. 111 and Madison Street]. This supposition is strengthened by the fact that in the memory of the old settlers at Roxana, no cemetery was ever located in that vicinity. Frank Smith, whose grandfather secured the Smith land, which was sold to the Roxana Oil Refinery, says that his grandfather secured the land from the government on a homestead claim, and that in his remembrance there was no cemetery there at that time. The fact that the bones are not those of Indians would prove apparently that the skeletons belonged to some prehistoric race, which evidently were later killed off by the Indians.

On numerous occasions specimens of the finest pottery made of pulverized mussel shell, and cemented with a substance, the nature of which chemists of today cannot duplicate, have been found in that neighborhood, and this lost art of mussel shell pottery is believed to belong to that prehistoric race. H. H. Clark, cashier of the First State and Savings Bank at Wood River, who is interested in ethnology and archaeology, went to Roxana this morning and secured a number of the skull and thigh bones found at the refinery. He also took along several well-preserved specimens of teeth found in the jaw bones, beside several specimens of the mussel shell pottery, which was found nearby. The find was made just inside of the Roxana gate, where six of the fifty houses to be erected for workmen at Roxana are being put for the foremen of the plant. At that place there is a small hill which rises up inside of the gate, and it was in the side of the hill that the skeletons were found. The discovery has attracted a great deal of interest, and many from Alton and Wood River went down to Roxana today in automobiles on learning of the finding of the skeletons. Many of the bones were taken away as relics and will be evaluated carefully.

Although the article describes the bones not as Indians, but of a highly developed race of people before the Indians, there were surely errors in this description, and the skeletal remains were Mississippian people. Other skeletal remains had already been found in the area. More importantly, the article does suggest that a large population did, indeed, live here.

Copper axes with portions of preserved wooden handles.

Many stone tools have been discovered in the area, along with artifacts such pottery vessels, including mussel shell type, used by Mississippians. Copper axes were even located toward the village center, implying that these people traded. A black stone mug and stone tomahawk were also buried among the skeletons. Seashells of various sizes have been found around the site, indicating that these inhabitants were part of a trade network. Some of the artifacts are on display in the Wood River Refinery Museum, which is located on the refinery edge along Illinois Route 111. Others were located to the University of Illinois. It is also reported that relics from the past are still found by workers at the refinery and kept as souvenirs.

Examples of a pipe and some of the ceramic and stone artifacts from several time periods found during excavations in and around the mounds at the Grassy Lake site.

Used with Permission from Cahokia Mounds

Artifacts from Grassy Lake Village, on display at
Wood River Refinery Museum (Roxana)

These artifacts were found in the area with close proximity to Grassy Lake.
They are on display at the Wood River History Museum & Visitors Center.

Photo used with permission.

MOUND DESCRIPTIONS BY MOREHEAD

MOUND 1

60 ft. long, 60 ft. wide, 4 ft. ht. Razed by Roxana Petroleum in 1918, No burials, but a red granite owl figurine, about 3 inches high, was found, and was displayed in the early refinery offices. Its location is presently unknown.

MOUNDS 2,3,4

50 ft. long, 40 ft. wide, 10-12 ft. ht. cone-shaped Razed by Roxana Petroleum in 1918; 50+ burials, some in sitting positions, but no known offerings. One was displayed at the Wood River Bank for a while. Current locations are not known.

MOUND 5

Unknown length & width, 9-10 ft. ht. 1923 Three badly decayed skeletons, stone pipe on head, some broken pottery, 10 arrowheads, 3-4 knives scattered throughout the mound.

MOUND 6

60 ft. long, 55 ft. wide, 3 ft. ht. 1923 One badly decayed individual near center. Early resident, R. P. Smith, described this mound as one of the low ones.

MOUND 7

60 ft. long, 60 ft. wide, 6 ft. ht. 1923 Three individuals with heads to south, A unique thick crucible with copper over charcoal and ashes, Fragments of a large pot on hard pan of burned clay with pottery fragments nearby, 5 in. spearhead and 2 projectiles near skeleton's hand, Evidence of mound base.

1 foot = .30 meters
1 inch = 2.2 centimeters

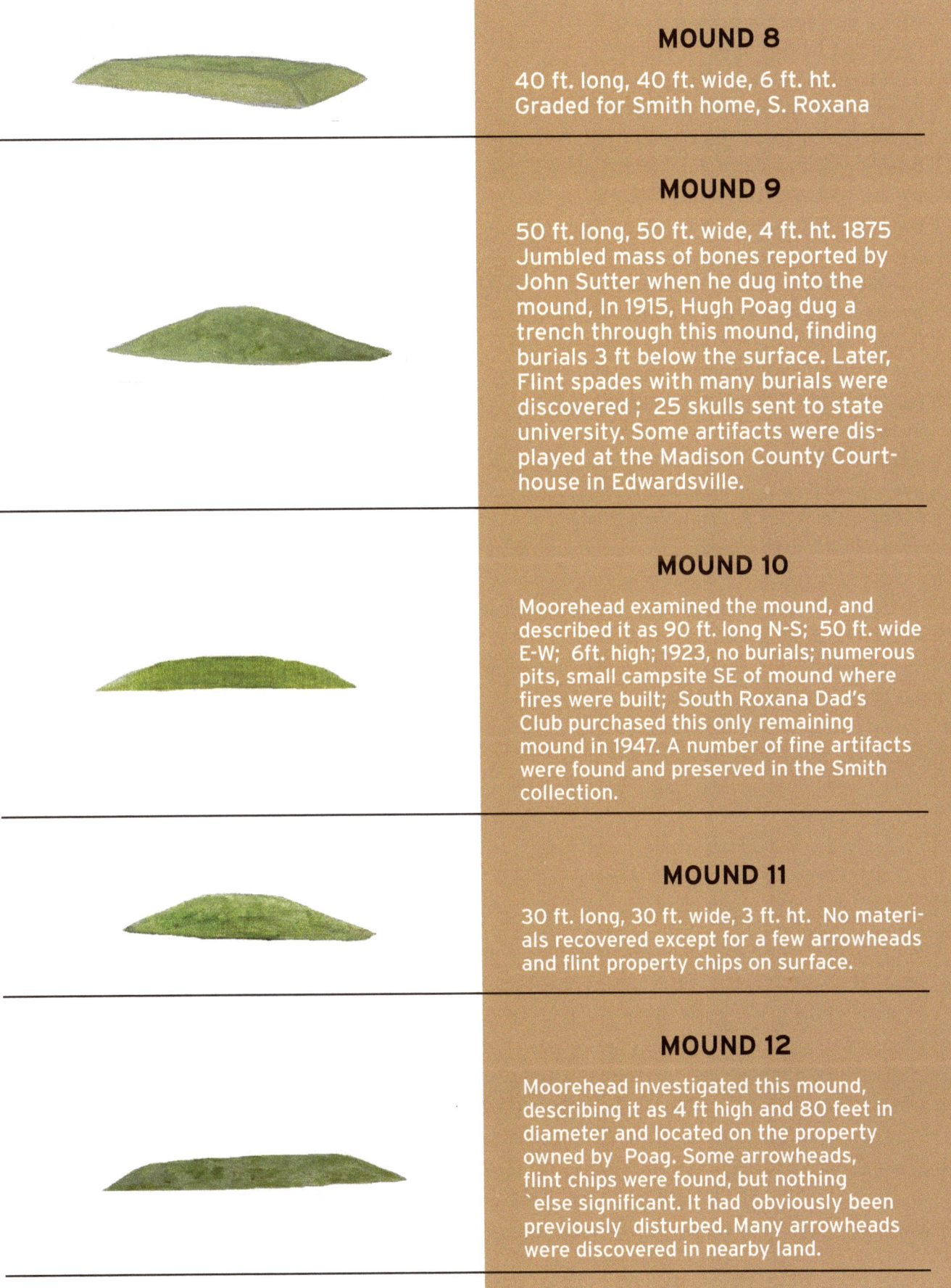

MOUND 8

40 ft. long, 40 ft. wide, 6 ft. ht.
Graded for Smith home, S. Roxana

MOUND 9

50 ft. long, 50 ft. wide, 4 ft. ht. 1875
Jumbled mass of bones reported by
John Sutter when he dug into the
mound, In 1915, Hugh Poag dug a
trench through this mound, finding
burials 3 ft below the surface. Later,
Flint spades with many burials were
discovered ; 25 skulls sent to state
university. Some artifacts were displayed at the Madison County Court-
house in Edwardsville.

MOUND 10

Moorehead examined the mound, and
described it as 90 ft. long N-S; 50 ft. wide
E-W; 6ft. high; 1923, no burials; numerous
pits, small campsite SE of mound where
fires were built; South Roxana Dad's
Club purchased this only remaining
mound in 1947. A number of fine artifacts
were found and preserved in the Smith
collection.

MOUND 11

30 ft. long, 30 ft. wide, 3 ft. ht. No materi-
als recovered except for a few arrowheads
and flint property chips on surface.

MOUND 12

Moorehead investigated this mound,
describing it as 4 ft high and 80 feet in
diameter and located on the property
owned by Poag. Some arrowheads,
flint chips were found, but nothing
`else significant. It had obviously been
previously disturbed. Many arrowheads
were discovered in nearby land.

Since written records were not recorded in the days of those who lived at Grassy Lake village, interviews with early settlers and reports from the days of refinery construction do give more vision to their existence. There were 11-13 mounds in a line along the ridge of the terrace, known as Savannah Terrace, and there are records of their contents. In 1921, Warren King Morehead of the Peabody Museum (Harvard) was commissioned by the state of Illinois to do excavations of Cahokia Mounds. In addition, Morehead's studies included other sites nearby, including the mounds at Grassy Lake.

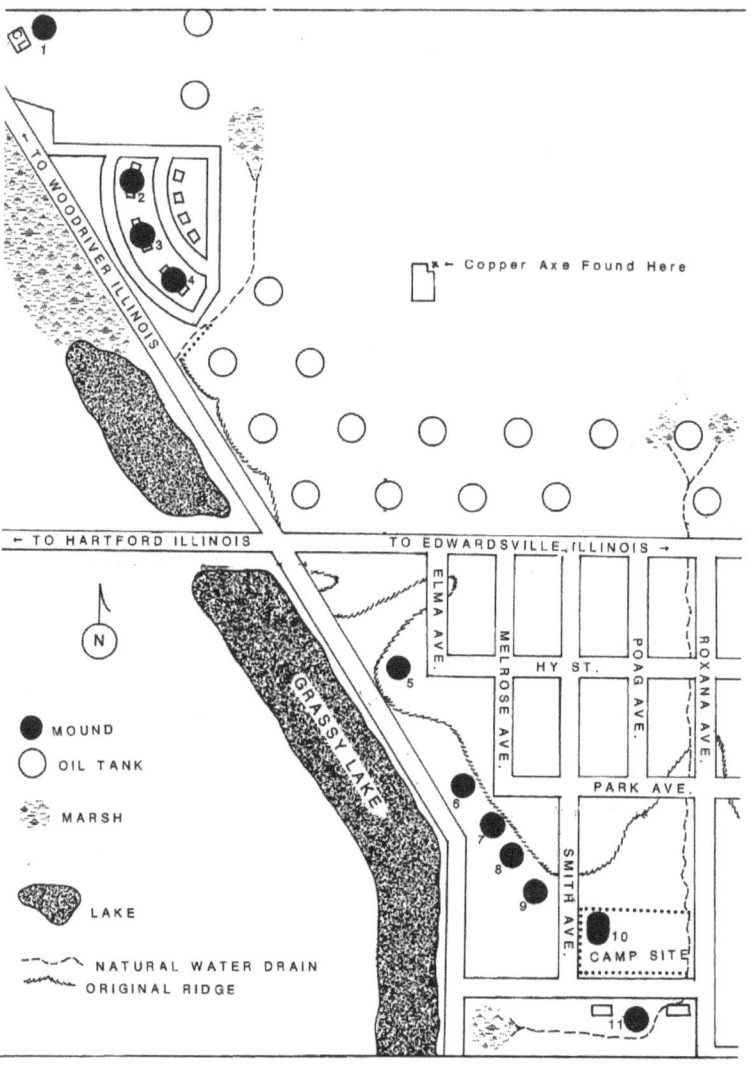

Map drawn by Charles Laun, Redrafted from Fecht 1951
The distance from the most northern to most southern mounds is approximately one-half mile (.6 km), with a similar east to west distance.

The refinery was becoming well established, making it nearly impossible to determine if other internal mounds were at the village. Mississippian villages generally contained a central ceremonial mound, so Grassy Lake Village certainly could have had one, also, and perhaps even others scattered about. Numerous Mississippian artifacts, including skeletons, have been discovered at the refinery site, demonstrating the importance of this village. Early Euro-American settlers such as Ray Smith, Hugh Poag and Charles Vaughn contributed reports of Mississippian presence in interviews. Remember that not all Mississippian people were the same. For example, Mississippians in the south would not have exactly the same lifestyles as those of the middle or north. The people of Grassy Lake and nearby Cahokia would be considered Middle Mississippians.

Some local folklore reports that there was another larger mound located near the present-day Wanda Cemetery in South Roxana; however, there were no excavations to verify this. Also, some residents reported up to 18 mounds in the area. Studies were conducted in the 1950's, 60's, 70's and 80's by museum and state university experts with findings of Woodland – Mississippian and even late Archaic presence at the site. However, with the formation of the refinery complex, it is nearly impossible to conclude that a central mound layout for the village was there. We can suppose that it followed the general pattern of other Mississippian villages with a central mound and plaza. Perhaps future generations will be able to do more precise investigations to uncover the secrets of the past.

This large mound, known as Schmidt Mound 11MS101, is located along New Poag Road just NE of the SIUE Baseball Field. The refinery can be seen in the NW background. There is another smaller mound located within the tree line behind the SIUE Baseball complex. Could these mounds be a part of the network activity of Grassy Lake people?

Artifacts from Around the Site

Early Euro-American farmers in the area have reported that in cultivating the land, traces of Native cultivation could be clearly seen before beginning farming in the pre-refinery years. Also, during farming numerous pottery fragments, arrowheads, spades, and hoes, some very large, were discovered. During construction of the refinery, an abundance of artifacts in the village location were discovered. When storage tanks were built, numerous pots were found, some whole and some broken. Many were taken to early refinery offices, where they were proudly displayed. As time went on, these items disappeared, probably into collections of employees. There is no record of where they are now located. However, there are reports that refinery employees have found many other items around and saved for souvenirs.

In writing about the site, *William G. Fecht wrote "Dr. P.F. Titterington, of St. Louis, has notified me that in his collection are two ceremonial banner stones and one copper axe. Dr. Titterington reports that there were twelve crescent slate bannerstones and eight copper axes found together in excavating for one of the oil storage tanks. All the banners were ceremonially broken. Mr. A. J. Throop (Amateur archaeologist), of East St. Louis, has reported three copper awls that were found in Roxana, and added to his fine collection."*

Mr. Smith, the previously mentioned landowner, found a bird-point near his home. Mrs. Lena Poag, another early settler collected items which were found on their farm. The Poag collection consisted of arrowheads, axes, hammerstones, a plumbob and the copper axe found inside the

site. When constructing the refinery structure, laborers discovered plentiful artifacts inside and outside the village location. Most were turned over to refinery officials. Many were donated for study. Among discoveries were numerous arrowheads, axes, and celts. In 1946, Shell Oil Company hired the Graver Tank Building Company for constructing a series of oil tanks, which would be connected to electricity and pipelines. While digging a ditch from tanks to inside the refinery, workers discovered numerous pottery fragments, along with other stone tools. In addition, a polished, 9.5-inch spade, one half inch thick, was discovered near a badly decomposed skeleton. Other workers discovered paint stones, wolf skull, corn grinder, and potter trowels. In 1948, a small, double bowl pot was found, perhaps a toy, which apparently had been molded with fingers. This artifact, along with others, were uncovered as deep as 8 feet., including a chalcedony spall knife. Nearly all of the items were given to researchers. The University of Michigan at Ann Arbor did analysis and reported that the items were a mixture of Late Woodland and Early Mississippian traditions. The university also classified the pottery into various categories. Descriptions can be found in Fecht's papers, with a copied located at the Wood River Refinery Museum. Most artifacts have passed hands through the years and probably ended up in collections.

Mississippian tools and artifacts similar to these Cahokia discoveries would have been made by people at Grassy Lake Village

Pottery fragments from Mound #5

Photos of Mississippian artifacts displayed at the Cahokia Mounds Interpretive Center. Used with Permission.

Life at Grassy Lake Village

Assuming there was a typical Late Mississippian village at the site, let us imagine the daily activity at Grassy Lake Village. No doubt, we would see similar events that were common throughout other Mississippian villages. The men, women, and children would all be contributing to lifestyles that would benefit their personal lives while contributing to the whole community. By the time Euro-Americans arrived in this area, the village had been abandoned, as was the big metropolis of Cahokia, which was named by European explorers after the people living there at the time, not at the time it was built and occupied. Since the Illiniwek Confederation of tribes spoke dialects of Algonquian, the people around what is now Illinois blended. Tamaroans were the people near the Mississippi and Missouri Rivers confluence, numbering around 3000. Many eventually migrated southward and joined the Kaskaskia tribe. The U.S. government recognized the surviving Tamaroans as members of the Kaskaskia tribe in 1803. In 1818, Illinois became a state with five leaders of the Tamaroa included in the signing of the Treaty of Edwardsville, where the Illiniwek Confederation conceded about half of the state to the U.S. Later generations of Tamaroa merged with larger tribes and ended up migrating westward to Kansas and Oklahoma.

Tool Making

The people at Grassy Lake Village would have needed tools for cultivating the soil for crops such as maize corn, squash, and beans. Stone hoes of various shapes and hoes made of mussel shells from the Mississippi River or shoulder blades of deer were used. Grinding stones for grains were made of various sizes. Stone drills, varying in size, were made. Even tiny drills were made for drilling holes into mussel shell and bones for making jewelry. Some were even used for recreation games.

Arrow points and spear heads were crafted for hunting deer, raccoon, opossum, rabbits, squirrels, and fowl were constructed for these hunters. The process for making the tools could be slow and tedious, but they were made expertly to last a long time and continuous use. Knives and scrapers were needed for cleaning the kills. There was very little waste – meat for food, muscle fibers for string and thread, bone for tools, large and small.

A few copper axes and vessels have been found at the village; however, it is unlikely that these were made on site. Instead, they more probably were acquired from trading since the Mississippians did have a network for trade. The huge city of Cahokia (named by Euro-Americans) had plenty of trade activity. Many tool artifacts have been found at the Grassy Lake site.

Photo of a toolmaker diorama at Cahokia Mounds; Used with permission.

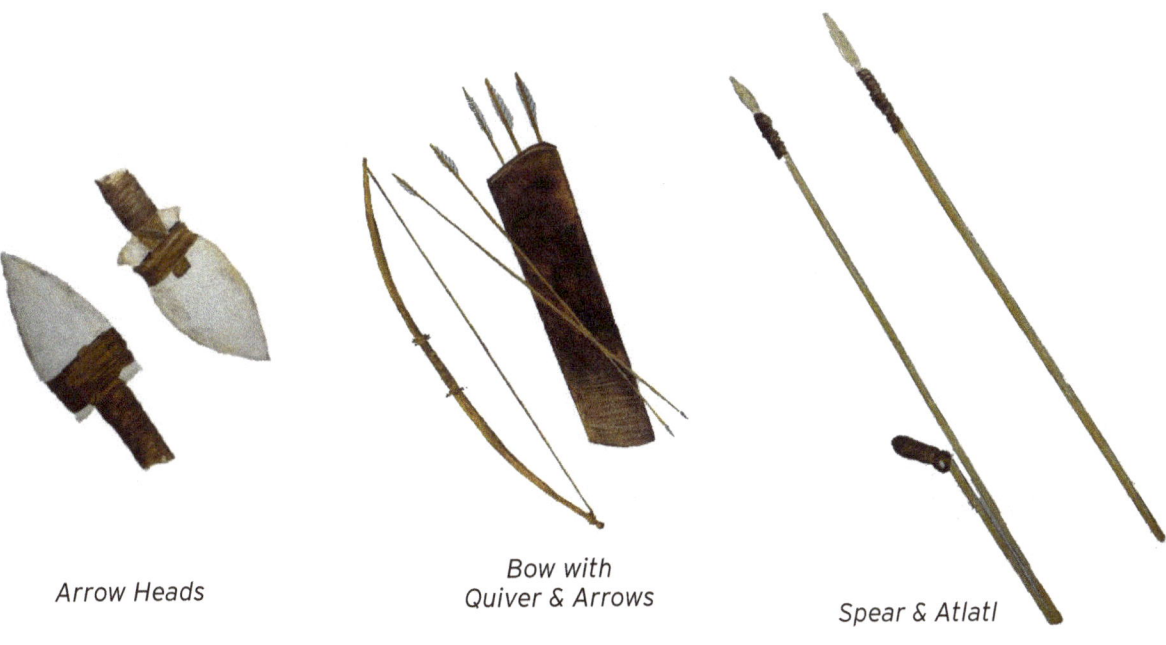

Arrow Heads

Bow with
Quiver & Arrows

Spear & Atlatl

Food at Grassy Lake Village

The location of the village was perfect for survival. Grassy Lake itself was a food source for the people, the nearby forests were another, and the Mississippi River, close to the west, yet another. There was plenty of game, edible plants, and good soil for cultivating crops.

...food from the forests

If you look in the distance east behind the refinery, you will notice that the landscape becomes hilly. These hills were covered with forests and all of the wildlife that comes with them. The Mississippian people in this region were good hunters, using the stone arrowheads with bows and spears. Deer were plentiful, and were an essential part of their diet. A deer kill would serve a bountiful supply of meat, which could be cooked over an open fire with parts smoked and saved for future meals. Nothing would go to waste. The internal organs could be ground and saved for food and be added to soup cooked in pots with other foods like corn, squash and beans. The furry hide could be used for blankets and coverings for floors or mats for sleeping. Smaller animals like rabbits, squirrels, chipmunks, duck, turkey, and quail would also be hunted, dressed, cooked or cured by smoking. Nuts like walnuts, butter nuts, pecans and hickory nuts would be gathered to add flavor

and use for snacks. Sometimes long poles were used to knock them from trees. Berries and fruits such as blackberries, persimmons, plums, grapes, wild strawberries, and pawpaws were gathered in baskets. The people had become experts for preparing food, and the nutrients from the meat, vegetables, fruits, and nuts would provide reliable needs for their bodies. The nearby flatlands were perfect for crops like corn and beans, and typical dwellings would have gardens nearby, allowing the residents to keep a close eye on intruding animals

...food from Grassy Lake & the Mississippi River

Recall that Grassy Lake had been formed from a remnant of the course change of the Mississippi River. At the time of Grassy Lake Village, the lake on the westside formed a boundary, and curved around to the southwest where South Roxana is presently located. Today, you can still see parts of it on the west side of Illinois Rt. 111 passing through South Roxana and Roxana. The refinery has built levees around parts to hold back water from the storage tanks.

The lake would have varied in depth from only a couple feet near the edge to 10-15 feet toward the center. Wetland plants like cattails, water lilies, lotus, arrowheads, spikerush, lush grass, pickerel weed, and algae would be common. These plants helped form an ecosystem that provided food, shelter, and oxygen for the fish, turtles, snakes and frogs. The large lake was a natural resource for food, water, and grasses for weaving baskets and roofs for homes. The people certainly realized the importance of Grassy Lake to their community.

Cattails must have been abundant at Grassy Lake, and the citizens put them to good use. The native people had learned to use every part of the plants and when time was best for harvesting. Leaves and stems were used for weaving mats and baskets. The fibers in stalks could be made into string for stitching. Toy dolls, animals, and canoes were made by soaking the leaves and folding into shapes. Even the fluffy seeds

were used to insulate foot-wear, winter clothing, and soft cushions. Juices could be used for salves and even eaten for pain relief. Mashed roots served as tooth paste and cream. Ground roots made flour for thickening soup and broth. Tender shoots were boiled to eat in salads or raw as snacks. Imagine the people, even children, working, wading into the lake to gather cattails for use. They were always careful to leave and plant new ones so there was always a good supply.

There would be fish, turtles, ducks, geese, and even some snakes at Grassy Lake—all used for food. People used nets cooperatively to make bigger catches, although individuals fished singly, also, using bone fish hooks. The nearby Mississippi River was also ideal for fishing. Hollowed log canoes would be used to venture into the depths of the river for bigger and more abundant fish types than from the smaller fish like blue gill, sunfish, and bass in the lake.

Fish Hooks

...Agriculture

The soil at the Grassy Lake site was formed by river bottom from the deep and wide rivers from the glacier melts following the ice age. The Mississippi River's width was from the hills and bluffs east and west of today's river. The flowing water carved out the river valley and left sandy, but enriched soil, easy for cultivation. The natives learned to enrich it even more with decaying organic material like fish and plants. Their cultivating tools made of stone and animal bones served them well. Nearby flatlands were perfect for agriculture.

Photo of Cahokia Mounds display.
Used with permission

Some native plants like chenopod, which produces seeds similar to quinoa and maygrass that has head seeds like wheat were sometimes planted to be ground into flour for cooking. Corn, originating in Mexico as maize, had become a staple food source for Mississippians, along with various types of beans, squash and pumpkins. Gourds, a hard-shell type of squash, were grown to use as utensils such as bowls and dippers. Large gourds were whitewashed and made into martin birdhouses. Martins eat mosquitos so they helped give some relief from the pesky insects.

Three Sisters Gardening

Family gardens were planted near homes, but larger scale agriculture was done in nearby fields with community members working cooperatively. You can imagine the hard work involved with producing and harvesting food for the entire population, and preserving foods for the long winter months.

All community members would participate in the ongoing endeavor.

Families often used the Three Sisters Method for gardening. Corn would be planted first in mounded soil, often with a dead fish, buried to provided natural fertilizer as the fish decomposed. When the corn was 10-12 inches (30 cm) tall, pole beans were planted. The beans would use the corn stalks on which to grow as they returned nitrogen to the soil being used by the corn. Squash, pumpkins, and gourds were planted around the outside, which helped keep animals away for the corn and beans. When white settlers came to America, the Mississippians taught them this good method for gardening. It is still often used today in American gardens.

Homes

Buildings in Mississippian villages were round or rectangle shaped, so it is reasonable to assume that Grassy Lake would use techniques for constructing homes and other buildings like all middle Mississippians. To begin construction, workers would first dig the floor a couple of feet (60 cm) into the ground. Next, they would dig a narrow trench around the outside to set poles for the walls.

Once the poles were set in place, the trench was refilled to hold them upright. Roof poles were attached to the walls and bound with fiber cord. The framework for the roof was steep to allow water to roll off easily during rain. Smaller, long sticks were used to weave in and out the poles and attached with twine to form a strong framework. There were no windows, but a door opening was made for using a woven covering that could be hung for privacy when needed. The woven stick framework was covered with a plaster made of clay and crushed shells. Thick bundles of long grass, thatch, was used to cover the roof in overlapping layers. Inside, platforms were made for beds, with storage space underneath. A hole was carefully made in the roof for fire smoke.

This was used only when necessary, since the dry grass could be a fire hazard. The people spent most of their time outdoors so fires for cooking were located outside. Homes were generally just one room about 18 ft. (5.5 m) long 11 ft. (3m) wide. However, larger public buildings were also constructed for meetings, storage, ceremonies, or even recreation.

Religion and Beliefs at Grassy Lake

Recall that Mississippians did not leave behind written records. What we know about these people comes from archaeologists' intense studies of the artifacts they left behind and even word-of-mouth reports from natives who knew the history. We know that these mound builders organized their society by rank, called chiefdoms. A chief, usually, but not always, male, held nearly all political power. Next, there were nobles, most often blood relatives of the chief, and the lowest rank were commoners, who had little or no power. They became ordinary citizens working as laborers, farmers, and craftspeople. The commoners gave a portion of their crops, especially corn, to the chief, who would have it dried and stored to use in emergencies when food was scarce. The people believed their chief was related to the sun, and even called him the Great Sun. The chief was given royal treatment with the finest home, clothing and food. The chief and nobles were not required to do labor, but served as the governing rulers.

Generally, there was a central flat top mound for the chief surround by a plaza that was used for ceremony and recreation. It is uncertain whether there was a central chiefdom mound at Grassy Lake Village since there was no archeological study. Early Europeans often

A Birdman Dancer, along with other participants was often used in religious ceremonies.

removed these kinds of mounds for agriculture, and after the refinery was built, finding evidence was nearly impossible.

It is reasonable to infer that since Grassy Lake people would have followed the same cultural patterns of other Mississippian communities, and that there was likely a central mound for the chief's dwelling and maybe a flattop stage mound on the plaza.

Mississippian and Woodland natives had a close spirituality with nature. They also were sun worshipers and believed that all animals contained spirits. They prayed to these spirits of the game they hunted for forgiveness. These people also believed that the world was divided into three parts — the upper, middle and underworlds. Sometimes there were huge ceremonies to honor the gods. The celebration ceremonies would be held with feasts, and costumes, masks, and dancing were prevalent.

Fire represented the sun on earth, so a perpetual village fire was kept, being extinguished, and relighted, only once a year for thanksgiving. In fact, they believed that if the fire went out any other time, they would die and the world would end.

These mound building people also believed in an afterlife. When someone died, they sometimes buried the person's belongings in the grave. When a chief died, his temple would be torn or burned down. His body would be buried in the mound, but new layers of soil would be added to it. The new chief would get a new temple on the mound.

Clothing & Fashion

Clothing for men, women and children at Grassy Lake would have been similar to attire worn by other Mississippians. It was very simple. Men wore a breechcloth, which is like an apron made of deerskin, woven cloth or other animal fur. The rectangular shaped pieces were attached to a belt

and covered the front and back. Of course, this simple clothing would not be much for staying warm in winter so animal skin and fur leggings were used along with a tunic type and cape covering. Often the breechcloth was decorated with dyes. Important people wore colorful capes and cloaks decorated with shells and bird feathers. Women also wore simple garments such as skirts and a sash. Jewelry made of shells and beads were used by both women and men.

Hairstyles: Men sometimes pulled back their long hair and tied it in a tail or bun. Often, they shaved half or front parts of their heads. The remaining hair could then be tied or decorated with feathers. Women usually wore their hair long, sometimes braiding it or using a headband.

Jewelry & Body Decorations

Tamaroans at Grassy Lake, like Mississippians in other parts of North America liked jewelry and decorating themselves. Women sometimes blackened their teeth using ashes, and rubbed colored powder on their faces and stomachs. Necklaces and bracelets made of shells, fossils, and seeds of various shapes, sizes, colors and textures. The jewelry and body decorations of men were often even more elaborate than women's, especially for special ceremonies. They decorated their heads with feathers and used face markings.

Sometimes men, especially warriors, even had permanent facial tattoos. Both men and women pierced their earlobes to ear large earspool ornaments. The chief often wore even fancier decorations such as ornate headdresses during religious festivals, setting himself apart from ordinary citizens.

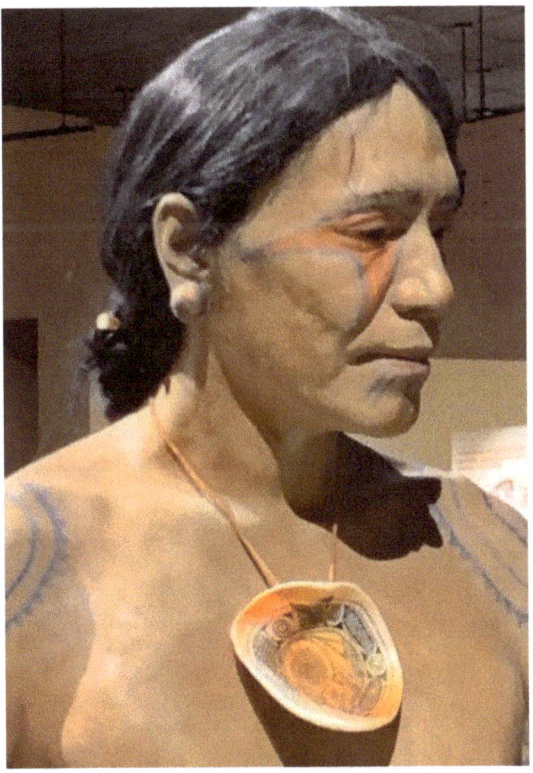

*Illustration Detail from Cahokia Mounds,
Used with Permission*

*Photos of Cahokia Mounds Displays
Used with permission.*

Mississippians had learned to weave textiles, using plant fibers, internal organ fibers from animals, animal oils for dye base, and even parts of animal internal organs for stronger fibers. A loom like the one here would be used for weaving textiles by hand.

Recreation

Like people of all cultures, the Mississippians at Grassy Lake would have enjoyed recreation games and having fun. Most days at Grassy were filled with people of all ages doing daily work and chores. Even children were expected to play an important role in maintaining the family and being sure there was enough food and supplies on hand. However, there was also time designated for having fun. Religious festivals would be held periodically with games and feasts. It was a good time for people to gather to enjoy each other and feel the excitement of contests and celebrations filled with music and dancing.

Chunkey One popular game throughout Mississippian territories was chunkey. It was played with a circular stone object about the size of a hockey puck with a hole in the middle. The game began with a contestant rolling the chunkey stone down a prepared slope made of dirt. Then players would hurl a pole carried by each participant. The winner was determined by which player's pole came closest to the stone after it came to rest. The game went on for hours until the players became too tired to continue. Sometimes players from various villages would send athletes to compete. Some villagers even made bets, using personal belongings. Each village maintained a designated chunkey field with packed soil.

Illustration from Cahokia Mounds Display   Used with Permission

Stickball Another popular game with intense competition was stickball. Although some southern Mississippians played with two sticks, Grassy Lake citizens would have used only one like others in the north. Playing barefoot, each player would carry a cupped stick, similar to a lacrosse one, about one meter long. The balls were made of hide stuffed with deer hair with a stone in the center and stitched together into a hard, spherical object that could be flung with great speed and power. There were no designated number of players as long as each team had the same number. Each team had a coachlike leader, who gave pep talks to the contestants. A goal post could be one or two posts or a pair joined with a cross bar. The games were played by men only, but sometimes a team of unmarried men would play against a team of unmarried women with the men letting the women win. The purpose was to allow young men to interact with young women in a courtship fashion. Some players became well known athletes.

Other Contests Sometimes, especially during festivals, there were contests for running races, throwing spears, jumping, shooting arrows, etc. Often there were contests for the children, also. It was not uncommon to see children playing with toy dolls, boats, or animals or just running around playing tag or similar games like children throughout time. Some board games similar to dice were common.

Art and Crafts

The next time you visit an art museum or other museum with Native American art on display, check out the exhibits with Mississippian art. The pieces you observe would be typical of the style made by Grassy Lake artisans. Certainly, the stone tools themselves represent artistic talent in their making. The precision of chipping away to make arrowheads, spears, knives, scrapers, etc. require exemplary skill. Polished hoes, axes, grinders, vessels etc. reveal the artistic talents of these people. Clothing, jewelry, tattoos, and other fashion items depict a recognizable style of Mississippian natives. They engraved shell pendants called "gorgets" with animal and human figures. Flint was used to carve ceremonial objects.

Pottery

Many fragments of pottery have been found at the Grassy Lake site. Lots of them exhibit etchings and rim designs, and it is known that Mississippians enjoyed painting on designs; however, paint fragments easily wear away, and only a few have remaining fragments.

Photos of Cahokia Mounds displays, used with permission.
Shells were used to temper clay, known as "gumbo".

Baskets

Woodland and Mississippian people wove baskets of various sizes and shapes. Stained grasses were frequently woven into them to create designs. The artistry styles of these people are unique to their culture.

Cropped photos from Cahokia Mounds Mural, used with permission.

Bluff Paintings

The great limestone bluffs along the Mississippi River are located just north of the Grassy Lake site. In 1678, French explorers, Marquette & Joliet recorded seeing bluff paintings by native Americans as they explored the territory, the first white men do so. Perhaps it is a stretch to suggest that Grassy Lake Mississippians participated in this endeavor, since the village had already been abandoned by the time Marquette and Joliet made their famous exploration travel up the Mississippi River. However, some experts have indicated the "Piasa Bird" paintings may have been etched and

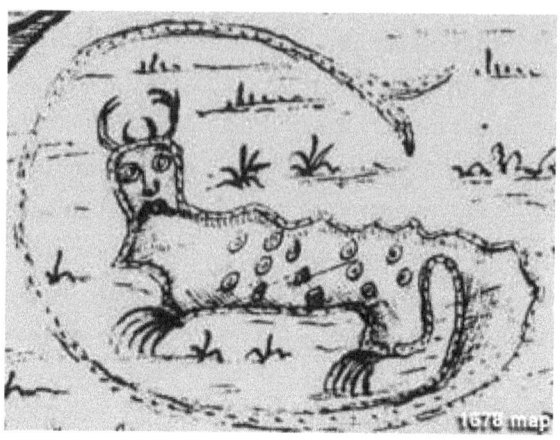

painted and repainted, around 1200 CE. So, it is possible that these Tamaroans or descendants could have participated in this artistic endeavor. Other, less famous, pictograph style paintings, also were painted on the bluffs by Mississippians. The creatures painted on the bluffs were still visible until the 1840's. Eagle Scout, Herbert Forcade, Sr. led an effort to restore the Piasa Bird painting in 1924, using descriptions from the journal kept by Marquette and Jolliet during their Mississippi and Illinois Rivers expedition.

"As we coasted along rocks, frightful for their height and length, we saw two monsters painted on one of the rocks, which startled us at first, and upon which the boldest Indian dare not gaze long. They are as large as a calf, with horns on the head like a deer, a frightful look, red eyes, bearded like a tiger, the face somewhat like a man's, the body covered with scales, and the tail so long that it twice makes the turn of the body, passes over the head and down between the legs, ending at last in a fish's tail. Green, red, and a kind of black are the colors employed. On the whole, these two monsters are so well painted that we could not believe any Indian to have been the designer, as good painters in France would find it hard to do so well. Besides this, they are painted so high upon the rock that it is hard to get conveniently near to paint them. As we were discoursing of them, sailing gently down a beautiful, still, clear water, we heard the noise of a rapid, into which we were about to fall. I have seen nothing more frightful - a mass of large trees, entire with branches, real floating islands, came rushing from the mouth of the river Pekitanoui (the Missouri River) so impetuously, that we could not, without great danger, expose ourselves to pass across. The agitation was so great that the water was all muddy, and could not get clear."

Such were the circumstances under which white men first saw this part of Illinois. The rocks, which Marquette referred to, were the bluffs which extend along the Mississippi northward from Alton. On the face of the bluff, just above the present city of Alton, were depicted the figures mentioned by Marquette, and with which we are familiar of the famous legend of the Piasa Bird [which is a fictional story]. Pioneers later recalled that when the Indians passed down the river in their canoes, they shot arrows or their rifle at the monsters on the bluff."

Pictographs on the Bluff above Alton

Why Was the Grassy Lake Village Abandoned by its People?

Let there be no doubt, Mississippian Mound Builders had built a complex and successful culture by any measurement. Grassy Lake Village, and similar villages were established with belief systems, economy, agriculture, government, and daily living, in place. However, by the mid-1300's these villages had been abandoned, including the grand city of Cahokia. By the time European settlers arrived, the Mississippian society in the villages had collapsed. It is known that many Tamaroans migrated to other tribes. The mounds, along with an abundance of artifacts, had been left behind, leaving us who follow asking why?

There are a number of theories for why this great civilization collapsed:

- **Overuse of resources**

Perhaps the Mississippians overhunted the game and used too much of the wood from the forests. Without these necessary resources, the people could not carry on the way of life they had established. Also, by planting the same crops year after year, the soil may have become deficient in nutrients necessary for successful farming.

- **Changes in Climate**

Another cause of decline might be attributed to multiple periods of drought. Without sufficient rainwater, crops would fail, and several years without water would reduce food production dramatically. Or maybe flooding of the rivers and streams would ruin the crops and affect the populations of wildlife game and plants. Or conceivably, multiple years of very heavy frost and cold temperatures affected animal and plant populations. One recent theory points out that maize (corn) does better in wetter climate conditions than dryer conditions. The "Little Ice Age" (about 1200-1500 CE) was a period of lower temperature and moisture, affecting maize agriculture. Evidence suggests that there was also decreasing human population during this time, so Mississippians may have been forced to disperse.

- **Disease**

A disease pandemic would spread quickly with so many people living close together. It is possible that viruses could have caused many people to become ill and die. With so much illness and death, the lifestyles of these people would be greatly distressed.

- **War**

Throughout world history, cultures have warred over resources, power, and ideology. It is feasible that Mississippian tribes competed, just as peoples of other times and places have done. If so, their energy would have forced a shift of values on how to use the resources they had. Loss of life would diminish essential manpower for daily living for things like construction, agriculture, and trading.

- ***All of the Above & Other Possibilities***

Most often, there is not one single cause of one historical event such as cultural decline. It is reasonable to conclude that a combination of causes contributed to the social decline of the Mississippians. Archaeologist work on an ongoing basis to piece together the clues left behind. As methods for soil testing, dating, and technology become more sophisticated, so does our understanding of the Mississippian culture and its development and downfall.

Photos of Cahokia Mounds Displays used with permission.

Regardless of what caused the decline of the Mississippian villages and cities, the story of their civilizations has not been lost completely. Numerous artifacts such as pottery, artwork, stone tools, etc. were left behind for future people to wonder and search for understanding.

Staple foods like corn, pumpkin, and squash are enjoyed by people throughout the world. You can be sure that the gifts left by these people ripple throughout modern cultures.

An Imaginary Trip Back In Time

Not all Native American tribes had the same naming traditions; however, typically names came from nature such as animals with certain characteristics that fit an individual. Some people received multiple names that could signify character changes through a lifetime. Of course, the names of the characters in this story are fictitious in English.

Since there is no machine to carry us back in time, let us take an imaginary trip to Grassy Lake Village. It is late spring, about late May or early June in terms of today's calendar. Running Fox and his people keep track of yearly cycles by observing the sun and seasons. He is 12 years old by these time cycles, and his two sisters, Little Flower 10, and Shining Moon 5, have been helping the family with planting and preparing for the seasons ahead. The daylight hours are getting longer and warmer now, and Running Fox knows these spring and summer days are the best to plant, hunt, and make each day count so they will be ready for the next winter ahead.

The village is alive with people doing productive tasks. Each person is busy contributing with jobs that will benefit their families and the whole community. On this morning, Running Fox has gone to the forest and prairie to hunt with his father, Eagle Eye. It was a good hunt. They were able to acquire three rabbits for the family to share as a meal. Eagle Eye is very skillful in using the bow and arrows for hunting. He has taught Running Fox to stalk a waiting rabbit quietly to avoid scaring it away. Eagle Eye tells Running Fox that later in the season, they will hunt deer, but only after new fawns have grown big enough to care for themselves. Running Fox's skills are getting better each day. In fact, today, one of the rabbits from the morning kill, was from his own bow and arrow. He is proud that he is gaining expertise in hunting. His father has been a good teacher.

After the hunt, he learned to say a prayer for forgiveness to the rabbits' spirits. They use a sharp stone knife to prepare the rabbit meat for a meal. They even saved the soft furs for his mother, Dancing Star, to use later to make a warm shawl. She will use the rabbit meat to prepare a large pot of stew for their family, including Running Fox's grandparents, Wise Owl and Golden Sun. These are his father's parents, who live next door in their home. They share most of their belonging and meals together. They have left a large garden spot between their grass thatched homes. They have already planted maize, yellow pole beans, pumpkins and squash, using the three sisters method. Most of the people at Grassy lake Village have similar systems for living. Their village has grown to over a thousand people. Running Fox loves these people. He has many cousins from his father and mother's families, and he has made numerous friends around the village. Likewise, his sisters have also befriended relatives and villagers. Children in the village often play together when there is extra time from chores.

On this same morning, their mother, Dancing Star, takes Little Flower to Grassy Lake to collect stalks of cattails. The stems of the cattails contain soft pulp this time of year, which is perfect to eat in stew and salad. Once they have collected bundles of cattails, they will take them to their home for preparation. The leaves are carefully removed and laid out to dry. They will be used for weaving baskets and to do repairs on the steep thatched roofs of their homes. The long fibers from stem skins will be dried and used for sewing and weaving fabric. Roots are also dried to grind into a flour for baking and cooking. Young Shining Moon, has stayed behind with her grandmother to help with making pottery and weaving baskets. Golden Sun is teaching Shining Moon some of the techniques. Today, she allows the young girl to make her own small bowl, showing her how to shape it and add a decorative rim. Shining Star even uses a sharp animal bone to engrave designs. Baskets of all various shapes and sizes have already been made for many uses. Today, Shining Moon has observed her grandmother weave a basket for collecting nuts from the eastern forest, nearby the village. She has stained some of the dried long leaves to weave designs into the basket. Little Flower and Shining Star are happy to spend time with their mother and grandmother to learn the flair for daily living at Grassy Lake Village.

In the late afternoon, the whole family ventures to the nearby fields to help with crops. The people of the village work together to plant food for harvesting. Stone hoes are used to till the ground for planting the corn, squash, and bean seeds, saved from last year's crops. Organic material such as dead fish are buried as fertilizer along with the seeds to make them grow better. They will take turns guarding the crop fields from intrusive animals. In the fall, the crops will be harvested, with a portion given to the chief, who will store them to use when food is scarce. A large thanksgiving ceremony will be held at the village plaza. Their chief will lead the ceremony, dressed in decorative clothing and head gear, including a wooden mask. A dancer dressed as Birdman will lead the festivities in dancing around the community fire near the Chief's flat mound with a temple on top. This fire burns night and day and can be used for villagers to relight their own home fires. Part of the ceremony includes putting out the perpetual fire; however, it will be relighted soon to begin a new cycle of seasons year of thanksgiving.

After work, the family returns home for an evening meal. The women have prepared dinner from leftover food from yesterday. The fresh rabbit meat is added to the stew to enhance the dinner. Once the food is prepared, they gather around outside the homes and share stories about the day's work. The children are happy to hear that their parents are planning a trip southward to the huge mound city, where they will stay a whole day or two. While there, they will be able to trade items for hard-to-find belongings. There are even things made of copper, granite, and shells from the ocean. These items have made their way to this great city (*now called Cahokia*) by a network of trading among other Mississippian and Woodland tribes. Running Fox had gone with his father and grandfather previously, so he knows well of the excitement for being there. This year, the family will travel by canoe on the great (*Mississippi*) River just west of Grassy Lake. Eagle Eye and his adult brothers worked hard to making several hollowed logs into canoes for their use. They are kept along the shoreline of the river. There are also some canoes along Grassy Lake to use for fishing in the deeper water.

As the family finishes dinner, the sun begins to set in the west. The food and settings have been cleared away, and they gather around the fire to talk. Nights are still cool so Dancing Star brings some blankets to use as shawls. The fire's warmth adds comfort, too. The firelight glows around the area, giving this part of their home yard a spiritual feeling. It is a good time to listen to their grandparents tell stories about their own adventures growing up and knowing their own parents and grandparents. Their grandfather, Wise Owl, is especially proud of their heritage, so he wants to pass along important history. The children listen well because they already know that it will be their duty to pass along the information to their own descendants someday.

It has been a long day, so the family decides to prepare for bed. Dancing star has brought fresh water from the lake for them to wash up. They go inside their little home to spread their mats for sleeping. As he reflects on the day, Red Fox smiles thinking about it, knowing he has done his part in making life better at Grassy Lake. He cannot know that the future of his people will include gradual abandonment of the village, and in the centuries ahead white settlers will change this site completely. How can he imagine that a huge industrial refinery with pipelines and tall smokestacks will be built over where he is resting right now? He is unable to conceive that the new residents will examine and study the mounds, tools, vessels, and lifestyle of the residents of Grassy Lake Village. But for now, he rests peacefully and thinks about tomorrow's new challenges.

Acknowledgments

Mounds, Modoc, and Mesoamerican   Papers in Honor of Melvin L. Fowler, Illinois State Museum Scientific Paper, Vol XXVIII

The Grassy Lake Site: an Historical and Archaeological Overview

John E. Kelly, Washington University in St. Louis, Missouri

Cahokia Mounds State Historical Site, Collinsville, Illinois

Bill Iseminger, Lori Belknap

Madison County Historical Museum, Edwardsville, Illinois

Wood River Refinery Museum, Roxana, Illinois

Wood River History Museum & Visitors Center

Robert LaMarsh & Alice Buzzard, Consultants

Julie Zimmerman, SIUE

Dr. Michael Montague, Advisor

Wikipedia, *various links*

About the Author

Ken Webster grew up in Calhoun County, Illinois, where it was common place to see Native American mounds among the hills and find artifacts in creek beds and farmers' fields. He is an elementary/middle school science specialist, teaching at elementary through post-graduate levels. Upon retiring from teaching in public schools, Ken joined the Cahokia Mounds Society, where his interest in local indigenous people expanded, especially when Cahokia sponsored a field trip to satellite sites of the great indigenous city of Cahokia. He was surprised to learn that the Grassy Lake Village was located on land where the present-day Wood River Refinery was established, in his own backyard. Thus, Ken gained inspiration to research and record a history of this important site with the writing of this book.

www.ingramcontent.com/pod-product-compliance
Lightning Source LLC
Chambersburg PA
CBHW041542120626
46551CB00019B/2807